DESIGN AND CREATE

Toys and Games

John Williams

GREGORY DRIVE SCHOOL
180 Gregory Drive West
CHATHAM, Ontario N7L 2L4

RSVP
RAINTREE
STECK-VAUGHN
PUBLISHERS
The Steck-Vaughn Company

Austin, Texas

Published by Raintree Steck-Vaughn Publishers,
an imprint of Steck-Vaughn Company

Library of Congress Cataloging-in-Publication Data
Williams, John.
Toys and games / John Williams.
        p.   cm.—(Design and create)
    Includes bibliographical references and index.
    Summary: Describes various toys and games
    and explains how to make them.
    ISBN 0-8172-4885-4
    1. Toy making—Juvenile literature.
    2. Games—Juvenile literature.
    [1. Toy making. 2. Toys. 3. Games.]
    I. Title. II. Series: Williams, John, 1939- Design and create.
    TT174.W565   1997
    745.592—dc21   96-48747

Printed in Italy. Bound in the United States.
1 2 3 4 5 6 7 8 9 0 01 00 99 98 97

Commissioned photography by Zul Mukhida

CONTENTS

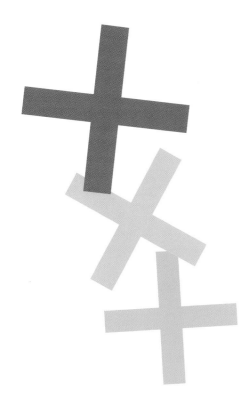

INTRODUCTION

Toys and games are things we play with. Some toys help us work out how real things work; others just keep us entertained.

Toys and games have existed for as long as there have been people to play with them. In museums, there are Roman toys that are about two thousand years old, and some of the board games we play today are like those used by the Ancient Egyptians. More recently, people who lived in the 19th century loved to play with toys that used mirrors and light.

A radio-controlled car is a modern electric toy that needs batteries to make it work.

These boys have made a game for themselves. It is called Nine Men's Morris and was played in Europe in medieval times.

What are toys? Look at the toys you use. Some are hard, like blocks; others, such as stuffed animals, are soft. Many toys have moving parts such as wheels and levers. Others do not move, but we can put them together to make bigger things. Many modern toys use electricity and are very complicated. It is often difficult to understand how they work or even how the parts fit together.

Some people buy toys and games. But there have not always been toy stores. For many hundreds of years, people made their own toys. Even today, some people do not have the money to buy toys, or do not live near stores, so they make things from what they find around them.

In India, kite flying is a popular pastime. People make their own kites from wood, string, and paper.

FLYING SPINNER

Making an object that spins around a point in its center can help it fly through the air. A frisbee is a toy that flies in this way. Here is a simple flying spinner to make for yourself.

YOU WILL NEED

- Several pieces of squared or graph paper
- Pencil
- Ruler
- Eraser
- Medium thick cardboard
- Scissors

1 On a piece of squared paper, draw the cross shape of the spinner.

2 Each arm of the spinner should be about 2 in. (6 cm) long and $3/4$ in. (2 cm) wide.

A helicopter has spinning blades attached to its top. A powerful engine inside the helicopter makes the blades go around very quickly. When the blades are spinning fast enough, the helicopter lifts off the ground.

NOW TRY THIS

Try making different versions of the spinner. You could make a bigger one or use thicker cardboard, or light wood (ask an adult to help you cut it). You could also try making the arms rounded, curved, or hooked at the ends.

Test them to see which one works best.

3 When the drawing is complete, cut it out and use it as a template.

4 Place the template on the cardboard, draw around its shape, and cut out the spinner.

5 To test your spinner, place it on the edge of a table. Make sure one arm sticks out over the edge. Flick this arm, very hard, with a pencil. The spinner should turn around and around and fly gently to the ground.

KALEIDOSCOPE

Kaleidoscopes have been made for hundreds of years. They are tubes with mirrors and small colored shapes inside. The colors are reflected in the mirrors, making interesting patterns. In fact, the name comes from Greek words, and means "beautiful things to look at."

Safety note: when you are making the kaleidoscope, make sure that none of the beads or glitter can get out and lodge in your eye.

YOU WILL NEED

- Thin plastic mirror (that can be cut with scissors)
- See-through plastic
- Small glass beads, sequins, or glitter
- Thick, flexible cardboard
- Scissors
- Pencil
- Ruler
- Masking tape
- Paper
- Glue
- Felt-tipped pens or paints

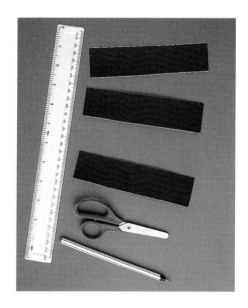

1 Mark out and cut three pieces of the plastic mirror exactly the same shape. They should each be long, but not very wide.

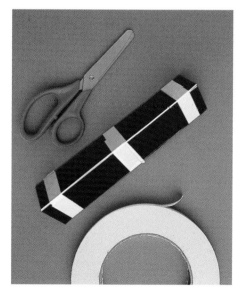

2 Use the masking tape to fasten the three mirrors together, making a triangle-shaped tube. The shiny sides of the mirrors should face inward.

Mirrors are useful in many places. People have them at home, so they can see what they look like. We also use mirrors in cars, to see the traffic behind us. Mirrors can also be used for fun, to reflect bright colors or odd shapes.

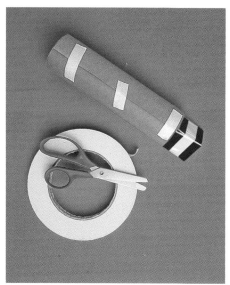

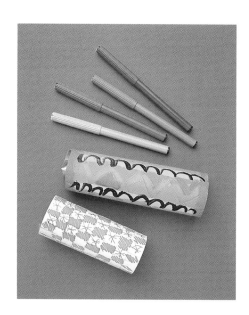

3 Cut out a piece of see-through plastic wrap and attach it over one end with tape. Put some beads and glitter into the center.

4 Attach another piece of plastic wrap over the other end with the tape. Cut a piece of cardboard the same length as the mirrors and wide enough to go around them. Roll the cardboard into a tube that fits tightly around the mirrors and tape it.

5 Cut a piece of paper the same size as the cardboard and glue it around the tube. You can now decorate the kaleidoscope with felt-tipped pens or paint.

MODERN WINDMILL

Most windmills have cross-shaped sails. Here is one with sails shaped like loops. This design is a very modern one. To make the sails, you will need to make designs like the ones at the bottom of these pages.

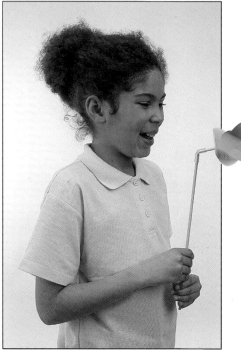

YOU WILL NEED

- Wooden dowel, approx. $3/16$ in. (5 mm) diameter x 18 in. (45 cm) long

- Flexible plastic tubing, approx. $5/16$ in. (8 mm) diameter x 5 in. (12 cm) long

- Tracing paper

- Sheets of thin cardboard or flexible plastic

- Scissors

- Pencil

- Tape

- Small hacksaw

1 Cut one piece of dowel 6 in. (15 cm) long. You will fit the sails onto this piece. Cut a second piece of dowel about 12 in. (30 cm) long.

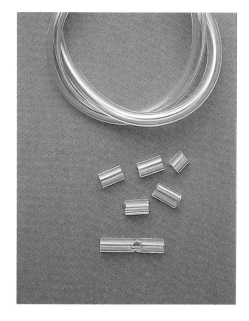

2 Cut a piece of plastic tube about 2 in. (5 cm) long. Make a V-shaped cut halfway along this piece. The cut should go almost through the tube, so that it can be bent easily. Cut five more pieces of tube, each about $1/4$ in. (1 cm) long. These are to keep the sails apart. Cut them down the side so that they will fold over the dowel.

Windmills can do jobs for us. Many years ago, windmills were buildings with big, heavy wooden sails on top. The wind pushed the sails around, and the sails turned a machine inside the building. The machine ground wheat into flour or moved water.

This modern windmill catches the power of the wind and turns it into electricity.

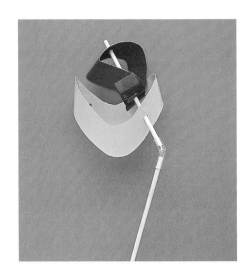

5 Put on the smaller sail the same way, then push the middle hole over the dowel. When the smaller sail is attached, finally put the middle hole of the larger sail over the dowel.

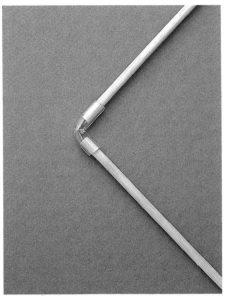

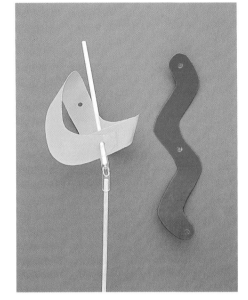

3 Push the two pieces of dowel into each end of the 2 in. (5 cm) tube. Don't push them in too far, because the piece of tube needs to bend easily in the middle.

4 Cut out two sails in roughly the same size and shape as the two colored outlines below. Make holes at either end and in the middle. Starting with the larger sail, attach the sails to the shorter piece of dowel. Put the holes at either end over each other to make the sail into a circle. Stick the ends of each sail together with a small piece of tape.

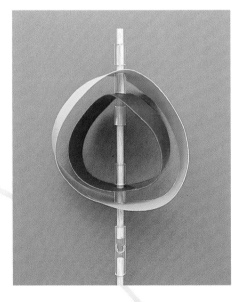

6 Put on the small pieces of plastic tube to keep the sails apart. Make sure that the sails spin freely.

DARTING FROG

Here is a toy frog with a sticky tongue. You can make the frog's back legs open and close so that it darts forward. Have a competition with a friend to see whose frog can catch the most "flies" with its tongue.

YOU WILL NEED

- Thick cardboard
- Thin cardboard
- Pencil
- Scissors
- 10 small paper fasteners
- Glue
- Paints
- Scraps of tissue paper

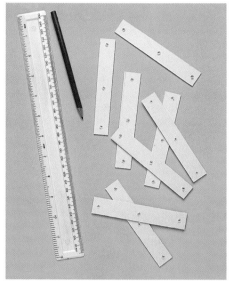

1 Measure eight pieces of thick cardboard. Each one should be about 5 in. (12 cm) long and $3/4$ in. (2 cm) wide. Cut them out. In each piece of cardboard, make holes at both ends and in the middle.

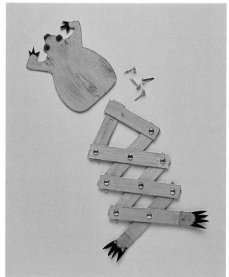

5 Also use a paper fastener to attach the frog's body to the legs. Put the body over the legs, then put the paper fastener through the middle of the last two pieces of leg.

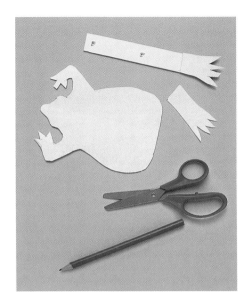

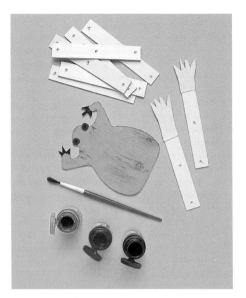

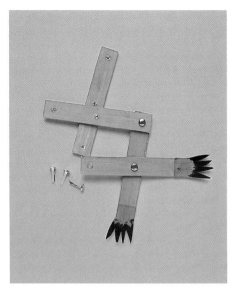

2 Using thin cardboard, cut out the back feet. Glue them to two pieces of leg. Also draw the frog's body. Give it a head, a tongue that sticks out, and front legs. Cut these out.

3 Paint all the pieces of cardboard that you have cut for the frog. They can be any color you like. Some frogs have spots on their bodies. Let the paint dry.

4 When the paint has dried, start to join all the leg pieces together with the paper fasteners. The legs should be joined in the middle and at either end.

6 Make some small "flies" from pieces of twisted tissue paper. Put a little wet glue on the frog's tongue. See how many "flies" you can catch with your darting frog.

Frogs have long back legs. The legs work in a similar way to levers to move the frog forward. This helps the frog jump quickly when it is catching food.

PAPER PARACHUTE

Parachutes that hold people are very large and need a lot of material. You can make a model parachute that will work just as well, but with a smaller load: an egg. See if you can fly the parachute and land the egg without breaking it!

Take care: you will have to drop the parachute from a height of about 10 ft. (3 m) to make it fly properly. DO NOT DO THIS WITHOUT AN ADULT'S HELP!

YOU WILL NEED

- Tissue paper
- Thread
- Small cardboard box
- Tape
- Plastic modeling clay
- Egg
- Scissors
- Ruler

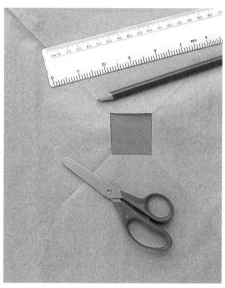

1 Cut out a square piece of tissue paper. Each side should be about 24 in. (60 cm) long. Cut a small square in the middle, $1\frac{1}{2}$ x $1\frac{1}{2}$ in. (4 x 4 cm). This will help the parachute float.

2 Cut four pieces of thread. Each piece should be about 3 ft. (80 cm) long. Attach one piece of thread to each corner of the paper with tape, pressing it on firmly.

Parachutes let people fall from great heights without hurting themselves. The material catches a lot of air, so that it falls slowly. Paragliding is a modern sport. People enjoy the feeling of flying gently through the air.

NOW TRY THIS

You can design and make various other egg containers. Use materials such as cotton, rubber bands, and pipe cleaners.

3 Find a small cardboard box. It should be a little larger than the egg. Attach the ends of the threads to each corner of the box with tape. Make sure the threads do not get tangled.

4 Take a piece of modeling clay that weighs about the same amount as the egg. Put it in the center of the box. Test the parachute. If it falls too quickly, you may need to make the parachute bigger.

5 Now it is time to try the egg. Take the clay out of the box. Roll up the egg in a piece of tissue paper. Twist the ends of the paper to hold the egg in the middle. Use tape to attach each end of the paper to opposite sides of the box. The egg should hang across the box without touching the bottom. You can now drop the parachute with its egg load.

PUPPET THEATER

YOU WILL NEED

- Large cardboard box
- 3 empty thread spools
- Colored tissue paper or fabric
- Cord or string
- Plastic modeling clay
- Glue
- Tape
- Ruler
- Scissors
- Pencil
- Paints

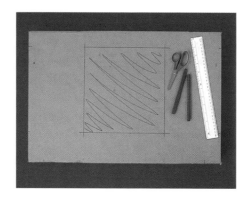

1 Mark where the opening is to go on the front of the box. Leave some space on either side of the hole, so that there is somewhere for the curtains to go when they are opened. Cut out the opening.

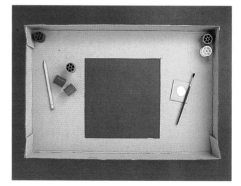

2 Turn over the box to the inside. Glue one spool in the top left-hand corner of the box, on the inside. Glue two others on the right, as shown in the picture. Keep the box flat and let the glue dry.

Here is a theater for all sorts of hand puppets. It has curtains that can be opened and closed during a puppet show. The curtains are held on cords that run over simple pulleys made out of thread spools.

Puppets are easier to believe if the person who is working them—the puppeteer—cannot be seen. A puppet theater gives the puppeteer something to hide behind. Adding curtains that open and close make the puppet theater seem more like a real theater.

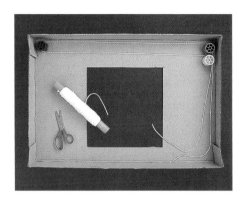

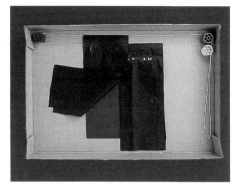

3 Thread some cord up the right-hand side of the box, over the spools and back down the same side, as shown in the photo. When you are sure you have the right length, cut the cord.

4 Cut two tissue-paper or fabric curtains. They must completely cover the hole. Fold the top over the cord and tape in place. One curtain should go over the upper cord and one over the lower.

5 Make two small balls of modeling clay and squeeze them around the bottom of the cords to act as weights. You can now open and close the curtains by pulling one cord, then the other.

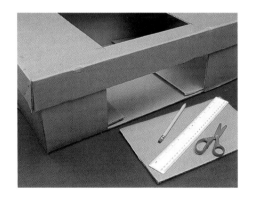

6 Cut a hole in the bottom of the box. This space is where the puppeteers put their hands to hold the puppets. To use the theater, put it between two tables or chairs, so that you can sit or kneel under the hole in the bottom.

7 Paint the outside of the box to look like a theater. You may also wish to paint a picture on a piece of paper to put at the back of the box, so that it looks like scenery in a real theater.

NOW TRY THIS

Make finger puppets out of cones of paper or puppets from old socks that will fit over your whole hand. Give them faces with eyes, noses, ears, and mouths made from felt or cardboard. Think of a story the puppets can perform in the theater.

JACK-IN-THE-BOX

YOU WILL NEED

- Tall cardboard box
- Scraps of cardboard, paper, fabric, and felt
- Square of stiff cardboard
- Ruler
- Pencil
- Scissors
- Paints, felt-tipped pens, or colored paper
- Flexible plastic tube, approx. 24 in. (60 cm) long
- Balloon
- Masking tape
- Plastic bottle

1 Make a "Jack" to go in the box. When it is finished, it should be a little shorter than the height of the box. Make your Jack look like a monster, an animal, or even something pretty.

2 Measure the size of the bottom of the box. Cut a piece of stiff cardboard the same size. Glue the Jack onto the center of the cardboard. This will keep it from falling over in the box.

Many years ago, children used to play with an old-fashioned toy called a Jack-in-the-Box. The Jack was like a doll with a funny face. It was put in a box with a lid. When the lid opened, a spring suddenly pushed out the Jack.

Instead of being moved by a spring, the toy here is moved by pneumatic pressure. This uses air to push things.

Pneumatic pressure is used in many machines. These men are working with a pneumatic drill, used for digging up roads. Air is forced along the hose, into the drill. The air is strong enough to make the drill work. It also makes a lot of noise!

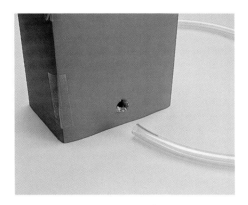

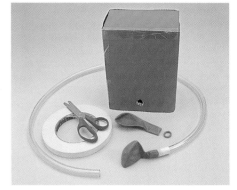

3 Decorate the box so that it goes with the Jack. You can use paint, felt-tipped pens, or colored paper.

4 Make a small hole in the back of the box at the bottom. Make it just big enough to fit the plastic tubing.

5 Cut off the lip of the balloon. Put the end of the balloon over one end of the plastic tubing. Use masking tape to stick the balloon to the tubing so no air can get out.

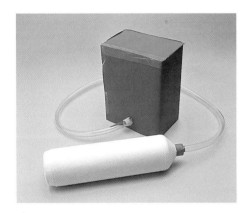

6 Push the other end of the tube through the hole in the box, so the balloon is inside. Put the end of the tubing onto the plastic bottle and seal it with masking tape if needed.

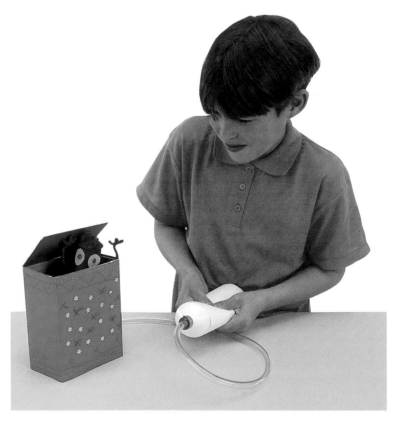

7 Put the Jack into the box so that it rests on the balloon. Shut the box lid if you have one. Squeeze the plastic bottle and watch the Jack rise out of the box.

BALANCING ANIMALS

Here is a way of making a toy animal that can balance on two legs or even on just one.

There are many possible designs for this toy. You can make it as big or as small as you wish, but it helps to start small.

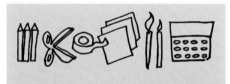

YOU WILL NEED

- Corks in various sizes
- Cocktail sticks or toothpicks
- Glue
- Tissue paper (optional)
- Thick wire (fencing or coat-hanger) approx. 12 in. (30 cm) long
- Plastic modeling clay

1 Make the body of the animal. Use a big cork for the body and a smaller one for the head. Make the legs and neck out of the cocktail sticks. Glue them in place.

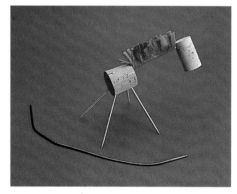

2 You can make the toy look more like an animal by gluing on features made from tissue paper. When the animal is finished, bend the wire into a curve.

Balancing is important in our lives. It is something we have to learn when we are very young. Babies learn to balance when they start to stand up. Then they can try to walk. Gymnasts and dancers can balance on one leg, even while moving very fast. When people have learned all about balance, they do it without thinking.

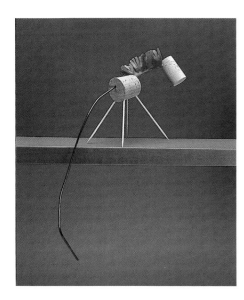

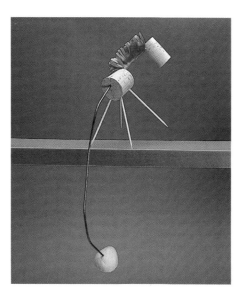

3 Put the wire into the animal so it is like a long tail. Then put the animal on the edge of a table or a shelf so that the end of the tail is under the back legs.

4 Put a small piece of modeling clay on the end of the tail. Move the tail or change the amount of clay, so that the animal will balance on its back legs.

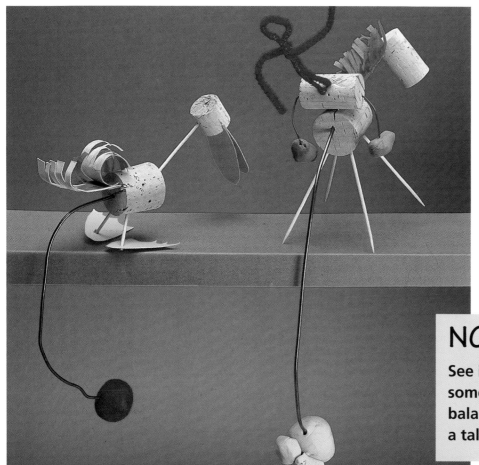

5 By adding or reducing the amount of clay or by twisting the tail to one side, you can make the animal balance in different ways.

NOW TRY THIS

See if you can design and make some other animals that will balance in this way. Try a bird or a tall animal with only one leg.

GAME SHOW BUZZERS

To make these buzzers work, use simple electrical circuits. Then you can play a game in your classroom —just like the game shows you see on TV.

You must make certain you wire the buzzer correctly. If it is the wrong way around, it will not work.

YOU WILL NEED

- 1 battery (at least 4.5 V)
- 2 buzzers (3 – 6 V), preferably with different noises
- Single-core electrical wire
- Wire strippers and cutters
- Small pieces of thin cardboard
- Paper fasteners
- Scissors

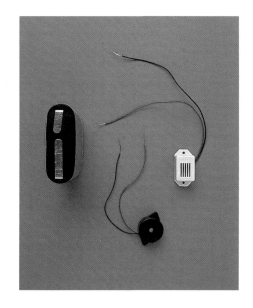

1 Strip about ³/₄ in. (2 cm) of the plastic covering from the ends of the buzzer wires. Attach one wire to a terminal of the battery. Take the other wire and touch the other terminal. If the buzzer sounds, the buzzers are wired correctly. If the buzzer doesn't sound, change the wire around.

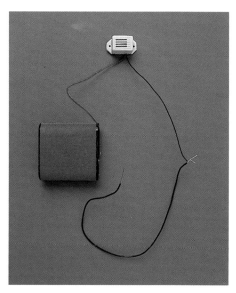

2 When you know which way the buzzers work, you are ready to make a circuit with a switch. Cut another length of wire and strip its ends. Join one end to one of the buzzer wires.

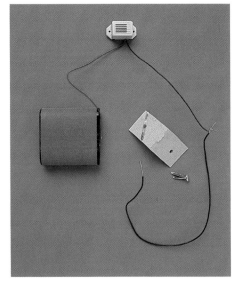

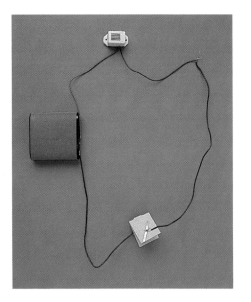

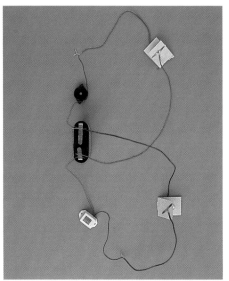

3 Make a switch for the circuit, so that it is easier to operate. Cut a piece of cardboard, about 6 x 3 in. (15 x 8 cm). Make a small hole in each half of the cardboard. Put a paper fastener in each hole with the points on the outside.

4 Cut another piece of wire and strip its ends. Attach one end to the battery. Twist the bare ends that remain around the pointed ends of the paper fasteners. Close the switch. The round tops of the paper fasteners should touch.

5 Now that you have completed one circuit, make another in exactly the same way, using the same battery, as shown in the photograph. You are then ready to play the game with two people or teams.

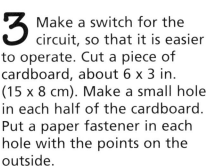

NOW TRY THIS

Now you are ready to have a quiz. Give two people, or two teams, a circuit with a buzzer and a switch. A different person should ask the questions. The first team or person to make the buzzer sound answers the question.

23

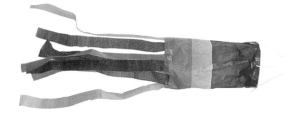

WIND SOCK

A wind sock is shaped to catch the wind. Pretty wind socks in bright colors can be hung in a yard or flown like a kite in the park.

This wind sock uses a swivel, so that its string will not get tangled. Swivels are used in many places: fishermen use small ones in their fishing lines, and sometimes huge ones are used on cranes so that their cables will not twist and break.

YOU WILL NEED

- Thin flexible wire
- Tissue paper in various colors
- Thin cardboard
- Tape
- Approx 5 ft (1.5 m) string
- Pencil
- Ruler
- Scissors
- Wire cutters

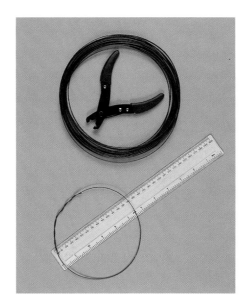

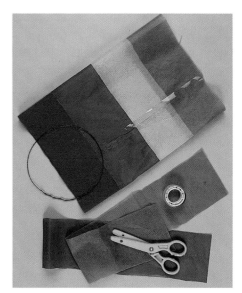

1 Make a circle out of the wire, about 6 in. (15 cm) across. Measure around the edge of the circle to find out how long it is all the way around. This measurement is called the circumference of the circle.

2 Cut four rectangles of different-colored tissue paper. The long sides should be a little longer than the distance around the circle. Stick the long edges of the tissue paper together to make one big piece. Then stick the sides together to make a tube. Stick one circular edge around the wire circle.

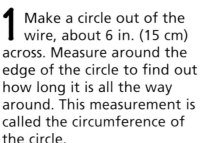

Wind socks are used at airfields to show the direction of the wind and how hard it is blowing. With this information pilots can determine whether the wind will affect their planes when they land and take off.

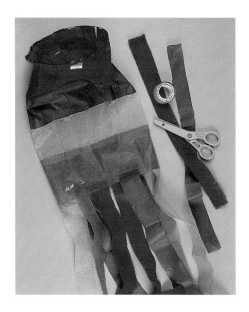

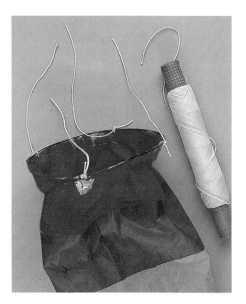

3 Make six paper tails. They should be long and thin. Stick them around the free end of the paper tube, with equal spaces between them.

4 Cut four pieces of string, about 8 in. (20 cm) long. Make a small hole in the tissue paper near the wire circle and tie each piece of string around the wire.

5 To make the swivel, cut a piece of thin cardboard about 1 x 3$\frac{1}{2}$ in. (3 x 9 cm). Cover it on both sides with tape, to make it stronger. Make three holes, one in the center, and one near each end. Fold the cardboard about 1 in. (3 cm) from each end.

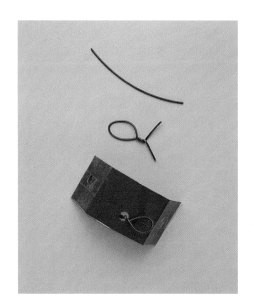

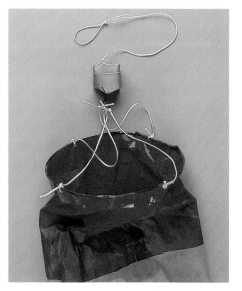

NOW TRY THIS

Wind socks can be all different shapes. You can try making ones that are long and thin or short and fat. Some may be cone-shaped or even in the shape of a fish, where the wire ring looks like its mouth.

6 Cut a piece of wire about 2$\frac{1}{2}$ in. (6 cm) long. Make it into a loop with twisted ends. Push the ends through the center hole in the cardboard and fold the ends out so they hold the wire loop in the cardboard.

7 Tie the four ends of string onto the wire loop. Cut another longer piece of string and tie it to the two end holes in the cardboard of the swivel. You are now ready to fly the wind sock.

FLAPPING INSECT

Here is a toy that moves like a simple machine. The insect moves up and down when you turn a handle. To change the movement from along the handle to up and down, you use a special shape, called a cam.

YOU WILL NEED

- Strong box
- Thin wooden dowel
- 2 stiff cardboard circles, 2½ in. (6 cm) diameter
- Flexible plastic tube, approx. 2 in. (5 cm) long
- Stiff cardboard
- Very thin stiff wire
- Rubber bands (optional)
- Scissors
- Glue
- Tape
- Paints or colored paper
- Small hacksaw

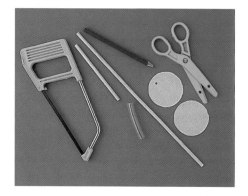

1 Cut a piece of dowel about 4 in. (10 cm) longer than the length of the box. Cut another piece about 5 in. (12 cm) long. Also make a hole in the side, near the edge, of one cardboard circle. The hole should be just big enough for the dowel. Leave one circle without a hole. Cut the plastic tube about 2 in. (5 cm) long.

2 Make a small hole in the sides of the box, about 2½ in. (6 cm) from the open edge. Push the long dowel through the holes. Make another hole in the center of the box, big enough to fit the plastic tube. Push the plastic tube through the hole until about 1¼ in. (3 cm) is left showing. Tape it in place.

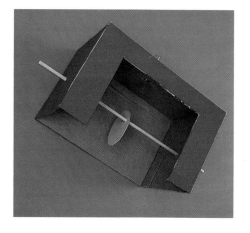

3 Pull the long dowel out of one of the holes in the box. Then push it through the hole in the cardboard circle, then back through the box. Move the circle—this is the cam—to the center of the dowel, directly under the bigger hole. Put some glue around the hole to fasten the cam to the dowel. (The photo shows one side cut out of the box.)

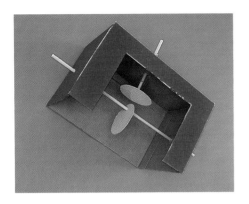

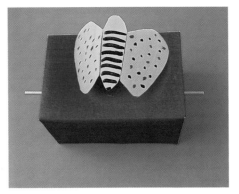

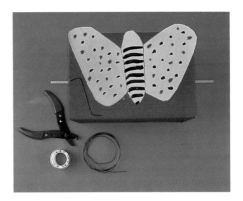

4 Put the 5 in. (12 cm) piece of dowel though the plastic tube. This will go up and down like a piston. Put the cardboard circle under the piece of wood and glue it in place. Let the glue dry.

5 While the glue is drying, make the insect (or a spider or bird) to go on top. Paint it to look as real as possible. Cut the wings away from the body and stick them back on with tape so that they flap easily. Glue the body in the middle to the top of the piston. Let the glue dry.

6 Bend the thin wire over at each end by about $3/4$ in. (2 cm). Use small pieces of tape to fix the wire to each side under the legs or wings. Attach the other ends of the wire to the top of the box.

7 Turn the long piece of dowel and the spider or bug will go up and down, flapping its wings. To keep the cam in the right place, under the piston, you may want to wind rubber bands around either side of the dowel to keep it from moving.

27

GOLF GAME

Here is a chance to have fun designing your own indoor miniature golf course. Use your imagination to make holes, bridges, tunnels, and obstacles out of recycled cardboard. Then make a simple golf club and challenge your friends to a game.

YOU WILL NEED

- Large cardboard boxes
- Variety of small boxes, tubes, cardboard, rope, or cord
- Thread spools
- Egg cartons
- Wood, approx. 48 in. (120 cm) long and 1/4 x 1/4 in. (1 x 1 cm) square
- Table tennis balls
- Glue
- Masking tape
- Pencil
- Scissors

1 Use cut-down cardboard boxes for each "hole" of the golf course. Leave a bit of the side around each edge, so that the ball cannot roll out of the box. Each box will need a starting point and a hole at the other end.

2 Make obstacle courses inside the boxes by gluing or taping on shapes made of wood or curved rope. You could also use empty spools or pipe cleaners. The aim of the game is to tap the ball through each part and down the hole at the end.

NOW TRY THIS

The aim of a game of golf is to go around the golf "course" with the fewest number of strokes. The person who hits the ball the fewest number of times wins the game.

  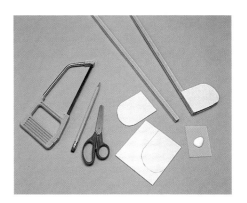

3 You can make tunnels from tubes or boxes. A bridge is a good challenge. Make sure the slopes are not too steep, and put a little wall on either side to keep the ball from rolling off. Glue these together first, then tape them onto the box.

4 Raise the box off the floor so that the ball can go down the hole at the end. Turn the carton over. Make a golf-ball "hole" from a piece of egg carton. Give the box "feet" by gluing an empty spool at each corner.

5 Use a piece of the wood to make a simple golf club so that you can play the game. Cut two "club" shapes out of stiff cardboard and glue them to either side of the wood at the end. Let the glue dry.

People play miniature golf for fun. Sometimes, the courses have different slopes to make the game interesting. Other games have a variety of amusing obstacles to hit the ball around.

GLOSSARY

balancing	Keeping a steady position, without falling over.
cam	In a machine, a shape that moves and makes other parts move around it.
circuit	An arrangement of things through which an electric current passes.
cone	A shape with a round base and a pointed tip.
designing	Getting an idea, planning, and sometimes making a drawing.
diameter	The distance across the center of a circle, from one side to the other.
energy	What enables all things such as machines or animals to do work.
flexible	Able to bend easily without breaking.
lever	A straight bar that is not flexible and that can move something by pushing or pulling.
load	A weight that something, such as a person, truck, or ship, has to carry.
obstacle	Something that gets in the way of something else.
perform	To do something such as acting or singing, watched by other people.
piston	A piece of wood or metal, inside a tube, that moves up and down. Usually found in an engine.
pneumatic	Describes something that is filled with or works by air.
pressure	The effect of being pushed or squeezed.
pulley	A wheel or circle, passed over by a cord or rope. Pulleys are used to help things run smoothly and to lift heavy loads.
switch	Something that makes and breaks a join in an electric circuit.
swivel	A joint between two things that allows one of them to turn around without turning the other.
template	A shape used to mark and cut out a number of the same shapes.
terminal	The part of a battery where other things—such as wires—can be joined to it.
transparent	Something you can see through, such as clear glass.
triangle	A shape with three sides.
tube	A long hollow round shape, usually open at both ends.
volt (V)	A measurement of the "push" or force, of electricity.

BOOKS TO READ

Graham, Ian. *How Things Work*. One Hundred One Questions & Answers. New York: Facts on File, 1994.

Lohf, Sabine. *Building Your Own Toys*. Danbury, CT: Children's Press, 1989.

McNiven, Helen & McNiven, Peter. *Toys and Games*. First Arts and Crafts. New York: Thomson Learning, 1994.

Oxlade, Chris & Ganeri, Anita. *Everyday Things*. Technology Craft Topics. Danbury, CT: Franklin Watts, 1994.

Pfiffner, George. *Earth-Friendly Toys: How to Make Fabulous Toys & Games from Reusable Objects*. New York: John Wiley & Sons, 1994.

ADDITIONAL NOTES

Flying Spinner Normal flight involves the forces of drag (friction), thrust, gravity, and lift. It is difficult for young children to design a working model when they have no experience of either the science or the materials involved. However, this toy is so simple that even very young children can be asked to make further designs.

Kaleidoscope This toy relies on the nature of light. Remembering the old rule that light travels in straight lines, children should be encouraged to explain why they see so many reflections from the three mirrors.

Windmill Most windmills operate on the same principle as that which creates lift on the wing of an airplane. Air moves faster over one side of the blade than the other. Making windmills not only enables children to study aspects of forces and energy, but also gives them a chance to think about the history of technology: wind energy has been harnessed since at least 2000 B.C.

Darting Frog This project demonstrates the mechanics of the lever. The basic aim of all levers is to move an object using the least amount of effort. It should be remembered that there are three types of levers:
1 The load at one end, the effort applied at the other, with the fulcrum, or balancing point, between them.
2 The load in the middle, with the fulcrum and the effort at opposite ends.
3 The fulcrum at one end, the load at the other end, and the effort in the middle.

Paper Parachute Parachutes are no longer simple umbrellas of material that rely solely on air resistance to float down slowly. With advanced technology they can now take very heavy loads and be so maneuverable that they can almost fly.

Puppet Theater This model will give plenty of scope for design as well as making. It is a simple structure, but children will need to make careful measurements, both for the curtain and to make sure that the theater is the appropriate size for the puppets.

Jack-in-the-Box Many mechanical systems work by the pressure of air or various fluids. Hydraulic systems, such as brakes of cars, can be very precise, but the power of controlled pneumatic systems should not be underestimated.

Balancing Animals The model should be able to stand evenly on its four legs before the tail is fitted. The tail, like that of many animals that stand on two back legs, is a balancing device. Children will eventually enable the model to stand on one leg. In principle the model is a balanced first-type lever, only vertical instead of horizontal. When balanced, all the forces are in equilibrium.

Game Show Buzzers Children will need to have had some experience with simple electrical circuits. This activity will reinforce any previous knowledge and help them understand the importance of sound wiring and the necessity for good connections.

Wind Sock This toy will be a useful addition to any project about the weather, where it can be used for wind direction and strength. It can also be used solely for decoration or even as a bird scarer. These last two uses will enable children to try out some good design work. The swivel part is a bearing that allows for 360-degree rotation, not unlike a wheel and fixed axle.

Flapping Insect The cam will not only move the piston up and down, but also can give it rotary movement. If this rotary movement is not required, then substitute square-section wood instead of dowel for the piston. This will fit through a square hole at the top of the box, and to make sure that there is no lateral movement pass the piston through a second piece of card about halfway between the top of the box and the camshaft. The piston should rest directly on top of the cam.

Golf Game Children can draw their own plans for golf courses—either miniature golf or the real game. This will not only take into consideration the size and shape of obstacles, greens, bunkers, and fairways, but also environmental features such as ponds and clumps of trees or bushes.

INDEX

Acknowledgments

The author and publishers wish to thank the following for their kind assistance with this book:
models Abdullah Crawford, Josie Kearns, Hugh Williams, Yasmin Mukhida, Rebecca Thomas, Tom Rigby, and also Cathy Baxter and Gus Ferguson.

For the use of their library photographs, grateful thanks are due to:
Eye Ubiquitous p. 11 (L. Johnstone), Bruce Coleman p. 13; Topham Picturepoint pp.15 and 16; Chapel Studios p. 18 (Zul Mukhida) and p. 24 (John Heinrich). All other photographs belong to the Wayland Picture Library.